GREECE

Designed and Produced by
Ted Smart & David Gibbon

COLOUR LIBRARY INTERNATIONAL

Introduction

When, in the early years of the last century, Lord Byron wrote of the *'Isles of Greece, the Isles of Greece, where burning Sappho loved and sung',* he was just the latest foreigner to fall under the influence of this fascinating, antique land, a place of sea and sky and mountain, which has conquered its conquerors for the best part of recorded time.

Greece has been a cradle of Western civilization for almost 7,000 years, from the time when the Minoan people were first established in Crete, that most staunchly Greek of all the Greek islands and, in legend at least, from long before that. Greek history, in recorded time, has consisted of a constant state of birth, decline and then rebirth as the Greeks, clinging to their beautiful land, were submerged in wave after wave of foreign invasion. In these struggles against the barbarians (which is itself a Greek word, taken from the *bar-bar* sound which a foreign tongue resembles to Greek ears) the Greeks usually triumphed in the end. It is some measure of their success that successive empires have come and gone, Roman, Byzantine, Turkish, all of which possessed their land and held them as a subject people, and yet the Greeks survived and have lived on to dominate or at least strongly influence, the character of their conquerors. The Greek language is still a cultural force even today, but then ideas have a habit of outliving empires, and it is in the realm of ideas that the true triumph of the Greek Nation really lies. This is not just because the Greeks have had a goodly number of ideas, but also because their underlying philosophy has endured and stood the test of time. The Greeks as a nation have succeeded in resisting alien cultures, while spreading their own ideas throughout the world.

To review Greek influence we have to begin with mythology. The ancient Greek gods came down from Mount Olympus and influenced the deities of Rome. The Greek city-states of the Golden Age are still regarded as models of effective government, which may or may not be true, but they worked. The architectural styles of Classical Greece, founded by artists such as Pericles, have influenced art for a millenium or more, and when to this we add the thoughts of Aristotle, Socrates and Plato, the conquests of Alexander the Great, the talents of Euclid, the plays of Aristophanes and Euripides, and consider what a profound effect these people and their works have had on Western civilizations, then it is easy to see why an understanding and love of Greek and Greece is still considered an essential attribute for an educated man. We cannot deny the Greeks their title to the role of a profound influence in the fields of art, thought, culture and letters.

To chart the recorded history of this land and its people, we must go back to the Minoans who lived in Crete and on the Greek mainland about 5000 BC. The Minoans were seafarers, who lived in stone palaces, had an alphabet and a significant culture and, after a long existence, disappeared completely, probably as the result of a cataclysmic earthquake about the year 1500 BC. Their existence was only fully understood after the excavations at Knossos, by Sir Arthur Evans.

The next civilization to mark the land that is now Greece arose at Mycenae in the Peloponnese, and reached its peak about the year 1400 BC. It was the Myceneans who, under their great king, Agamemnon, attacked Troy and caused the struggle immortalised by Homer, but the ten year struggle exhausted Mycenean power and the land fell to a new invader, the Dorians, fierce warriors from the Balkans who brought the Dark Ages to Greece. The ruins of Mycenae were excavated by Schliemann in 1876, and the treasures he found are now in the National Museum at Athens. The Dorians captured Mycenae about 1400 BC, and extinguished their culture, and so began a period which lasted for over 400 years but which led to the Age of the *polis,* or 'city-state', which flourished from about 800 BC. It was this period which created the Greece that the world remembers and admires today. This was the age of the great cities of Athens, Corinth, Thebes, Sparta and Sicyon, each with its own culture and government, but the inhabitants were linked as Greeks and by the introduction of such events as the Olympic Games, which began in 776 BC. In about 500 BC the Golden Age began, and Greek culture reached its peak. This too was the *Classical Age*; the time of Pericles, Sophocles, Aeschylus and Herodotus, the father of history, who told us much of what we know about the Ancient world. These were the men who built the Acropolis: introduced, albeit briefly, democratic government, and left posterity with a rich heritage of art and ideas.

That one small region could, in one short time, produce these men, and many others such as Xenophon, Aristotle and Thucydides, is in itself remarkable, but this growth in culture was accompanied by the expansion of the Greek states which brought them into conflict with the Persian Empire of Xerxes, who was eventually defeated at Salamis and Marathon, an heroic time in which the stand of Leonidas and his Spartans at Thermopylae has been chiefly remembered.

However, the unity of the Greeks couldn't last, for even today Greeks love a good argument, and after combining to defeat the Persians, the states began to quarrel among themselves. The Peloponnesian War between Athens and Sparta lasted for nearly thirty years, after Sparta, always the most warlike of the city states, declared against the intellectual tyranny of Athens. The war led to the fall of Athens as a dominant power in the peninsula.

As with the Dorian invasion, which ushered in the Dark Ages, rejuvenation came from the north; from Macedonia, in the person of Philip of Macedon, who invaded the South of Greece in 338 BC, overthrew the city states and attempted to establish himself as dictator. Philip needed the men of the South to join his armies for further wars against the Persians, but he died young and left the twin tasks in the capable hands of his mighty son, Alexander. Alexander was certainly one of the greatest generals who ever lived and his father had added to his natural abilities with the benefits of an expensive education, hiring Aristotle as his tutor. Alexander had an insatiable lust for conquest, and in his short reign he conquered Libya and Babylon, destroyed the Persian empire and marched as far as India before he died, lamenting that there were no more worlds to conquer. He had thus spread Greek civilization, by force of arms, over much of the then known world.

Alexander, for all his talents, was a dictator, and with his death the Greeks again threw off the yoke of kings and the second great period, the *Hellenistic Age,* saw the creation of even more wonders, among them the construction of the Colossus of Rhodes, one of the Wonders of the Ancient World.

All civilizations decline, and a taste for luxury and a neglect of arms destroyed the glory of the Greeks. Around the year 200 BC the Greeks met a new and more subtle enemy, in the expanding power of the people of Rome, and in AD 146 Corinth fell to the Roman legions. Greece became a Roman province and remained so until the Roman empire was divided into two halves in AD 340. Greek ideas though, did not die, and Athens was the cultural centre of the Roman world. By this time Rome had become Christian, and after partition the Greek Church became part of the Eastern Church and the country itself was ruled by the Byzantine emperors who governed from Constantinople, a fact which, largely through the influence of the Greek Orthodox Church, has endowed Greece with many imposing Byzantine churches, all containing beautiful frescoes and icons. The black-garbed Orthodox priest, with his deep beard and stovepipe hat, is a common sight in all Greek towns and villages where he wields as much, or even more, power than the elected mayor.

In 1200 the Byzantine Empire also fell, this time to Western

The Parthenon, or Temple of Athena Polias left, the loftiest building on the Acropolis, Athens.

Overleaf: *the floodlit Acropolis during one of the summer Sound and Light (Son et Lumière) performances.*

Crusaders in the pay of the Venetians. The Crusaders sacked Constantinople in 1204 and the Venetians took the Ionian Islands as their prize. Later, in 1304, the Knights of St John of Jerusalem established themselves on the island fortress of Rhodes, but the Greeks lived on in the mainland, and continued to cherish their own land and language.

None could resist the rising power of the next empire to engulf the Greek homeland, the Turks, who came from the East in overwhelming force and with the impetus of a new creed, Islam.

Constantinople fell to the Ottoman Turks in 1453 and Athens, three years later in 1456. The Turks ruled Greece for the next four hundred years, a stagnant period, frequently interrupted by struggles for Greek independence, but in which, as a result of the Turkish presence, Greek culture escaped the Italianate influence of the Renaissance. Greece re-emerged as a nation in the early nineteenth century. The English Lord Byron is well remembered in Greece for his part in the struggle which followed the Declaration of Independence in 1821, and a British Admiral, Codrington, led the allied fleet which destroyed the Turkish Navy at Navarino in 1827. Greece, once free from Turkish rule, became a monarchy, but Corfu was ruled by the British until 1864, and Crete and Samos were retained by the Turks until eventually the Cretans rose in rebellion and drove them out. Greece fought against Turkey again in the Great War of 1914-18 and won, but was over-run in the Second World War by the Italians and the Germans. No sooner was that conflict over than Civil War broke out and peace only finally returned to the country in 1949. The years since have seen disagreements with Britain and Turkey over the question of Cyprus, the rejection of the monarchy and the unhappy rule of a military junta. Today though, Greece again enjoys democratic government and is an associate member of the European Economic Community, a nation rich in agricultural and commercial resources, while still retaining that cultural heritage inherited from a noble and antique past.

Looking back from this point, over the long, tumultuous history of the Greeks, several strands emerge, which need to be picked out from the whole, for they illustrate the fundamentals of the Greek Nation of today. The enduring success of the Greeks has been in the realm of ideas, which have fostered the awareness of the Greek identity. Then, there has been the ability to go on being Greek, *as a nation,* whatever alien power has occupied their territory. When foreign power eventually declined, even after hundreds of years, the Greeks arose again and continued as before, as a race, a people, a nation.

Foreign occupation certainly has influenced the Greeks, and there are echoes of the Italians and British in the Ionian islands, and of the Turks almost everywhere, but thanks to their vast store of inherited culture, the Greeks have resisted that Balkanization which debilitated the nations to their immediate north.

The Greeks are travellers still and, enjoying travel, are hospitable to strangers. In terms of Europe, Greece is a poor country, with agriculture as the main source of livelihood. Manufacturing industry, apart from a few large modern companies, is often conducted on a very small scale. Tourism is essential to the Greek economy and has boomed since the 1950s, a fact which is largely due to the low cost of living, the excellent weather and the engaging character of the Greek people, who have managed to survive the massive tourist impact without turning sour.

Fortunately, although not particularly large – at just over 50,000 square miles about the size of England – the Greek landscape is remarkably varied, and the tourists can spread themselves out fairly thinly all over the mainland and among the hundreds of islands off the coast. Of the country's estimated population of nine million, more than two million live in Athens and the immediate neighbourhood, so the country leaves the visitor with a sense of space, a land lit by translucent light, and never far from the sea. Greece has been called *a*

The sun-baked houses of Fira left cluster in terraces on Santorini (Thira), the most important island of the Southern Sporades.

Begun c. 437-432 B.C., the monumental gateway of the Propylaea overleaf on the Acropolis, was left unfinished at the beginning of the Peloponnesian War.

land of mountains and sea, and much of the land stands at over 3,000 feet, which is certainly mountainous; Mount Olympus, the highest mountain, is 9,550 feet high. Fingers of land poke out into the sea in long peninsulas, which, with their tips submerged, carry on into the waters in a string of islands.

Climatically, Greece is equally well favoured with hot summers and all the hallmarks of the Mediterranean, but the mountainous nature of the land causes much local variation. Greece has ski-resorts and ample snow, so if the pervading influence of the sea tempers the worst effects of the Balkans, the winters in the hills can be bitterly cold, and the summers – notably during July and August – very warm indeed.

The Greeks are naturally very proud of their land, famed as it is for beauty and culture. The visitor will soon see why, for Greece is one country which really lives up to its far-flung reputation. The skies are blue, the hills green and gold, the houses a pure white, and it all sparkles in the sunshine. When the visitor eventually leaves, it is with great reluctance, and a vow to return again soon – and again and again, to sample a little more of the glory that is Greece.

ENTERTAINMENT

Greece can never be dull. The people see to that, both the locals who are never less than themselves, and therefore unique, and the tourists who in this most relaxed of countries, can always enjoy themselves. In the daytime there are sights to see, temples, palaces and museums to visit, and always the sea, for boating, sailing, fishing or swimming. Beaches are carpeted with browning visitors and in the bars the conversation is incessant. Inland there is golf, tennis, riding, and everywhere the need to recover from the night before and prepare for the evening ahead. In Greece the nightlife is as varied as the land itself. For the Greeks, entertainment is found in the cafés and tavernas, gathering in groups, usually almost exclusively male groups, to argue the issues of the day until late into the night. A television blares out in every café, but no one watches anything but football. This is café society, small and friendly, but for the visitor, who will soon feel at home in this noisy, relaxed, masculine atmosphere, there are literally hundreds of small discos and tavernas where the music and dancing goes on until the dawn, and the drink prices are half those asked in the more elegant haunts peopled exclusively by visitors. Bouzouki music is plucked out over the ouzo, and after a while the men will rise and dance the *Sirtaki,* the great folk dance of Greece, which visitors should just watch unless they can do it quite well.

In the larger towns, the entertainment is more varied. Cinemas showing foreign films with Greek sub-titles are popular, and since you eat late in Greece you can take in a show, eat afterwards and then go on to a disco without any problem. Classical plays, for the culturally-minded, can also be found on the ancient sites, but you need a good command of Greek to follow plots which largely feature rape, incest and murder. Son-et-Lumière shows are also popular. Culture apart, and the basic attractions of bar and taverna accepted as a standard feature, the traveller must choose his destination with care. Night clubs are expensive and poor value. Athens is a large, cosmopolitan city, and can offer as wide a choice of nightlife as any capital in Europe. The old part of Athens, the Plaka, is the area to visit, but nothing much happens there before 10 p.m. There are nearly 300 open-air cinemas, a National Theatre and an Opera, and hundreds of restaurants at all prices offering everything from French cuisine to typical local dishes. Indeed, the Greeks usually infiltrate local dishes into even the most sophisticated menu, and the wine, resinated or not, is usually Greek, frequently good and always cheap. If you enjoy folklorique dances, the Dora Stratou theatre stages them every evening.

In the countryside and on the islands, the entertainment available varies according to the place, and the availability of tourists. Few people realise that there is snow on the mountains of Greece and good skiing on Mount Pelion, but Greece, above all, is a summer country. Spetsai, a popular resort in the Saronic islands, south and west of Athens, is the place to go for entertainment, and can serve as a good example of nightlife on an island. During the daytime there is the usual range of activities; swimming, sailing, snorkelling, windsurfing and admiring the girls, but as dusk falls, the island,

13

ΟΔΙ
ΟC

CΠ ΡΙΔΟΝ

14

which is very small, really starts to jump.

Evening in Spetsai begins with a stroll along the Dappia, a long promenade by the harbour, a street fronted by the sea and backed by bars. The evening air is heavy with cigarette smoke and the scent of *ouzo*. After an hour or two here you go on to eat, at any time up to midnight, in one of the hundred restaurants and tavernas in the town, before moving on to a disco or a bar with dancing. Perhaps from time to time in the course of the evening there is a little folklorique dancing exhibition by the men. More often the time passes in good, noisy, enjoyable company, visitors and locals mixing together.

Mykonos, a beautiful island and always a popular place for artists and writers, has developed into the most popular centre of the Cyclades. By day, stroll amid the fascinating maze of small, narrow streets within its ancient town; visit the myriad chapels that are scattered throughout, or bask in the sun on one of the large remote, silky beaches. Then, when dusk falls, sample the nightlife – its variety is renowned.

Ios, another island in the Cyclades, is different again; barren, hot, made exotic by its very nature, but very beautiful. Ios is a fashionable place to go to, and very much on the way up as a holiday destination, but chiefly noted historically as the place where Homer died.

So, how do you enjoy yourself in Greece? You relax, soak up the sun, drink a little *ouzo,* and don't hurry or worry. The evenings are long and the nights longer, so linger over the meal, stay on to hear the bazouki music and the old Greek songs, and so capture the flavour that is Greece.

GETTING ABOUT

The Greeks are great rovers, the most famous seafaring nation of Ancient times. They live in a land which, if not large, is still very diffused, and it is surprising to discover that travelling about in Greece is as easy and pleasant as just staying in one spot and soaking up the sun. Pleasant, easy, inexpensive – yes – but adventurous. Nothing in Greece goes *quite* according to plan, so if you aim to tour around and see a lot of the country, a little patience will take you a very long way. On the other hand, your fellow Greek travellers will be friendly and such a trip can never be dull.

The National Tourist Organization (NTOG) has offices in all main Greek cities, and Greece has one particularly useful institution in the men of the Tourist Police. They are more like guides than policemen and are solely concerned with helping tourists. They are multi-lingual, and wear badges to indicate the languages they speak. The Tourist Police operate all over the country, are always obliging, and have a deep knowledge of their local district.

Communications within Greece are very good, if somewhat erratic, but the buses are notably efficient, outside of Crete. Bus seats can and should be reserved in advance. The country buses are somewhat ancient and usually full of old ladies and the occasional goat. The island groups are linked by ferries, which are in themselves entertaining and an ideal way to travel. Accommodation of all kinds is available, but camping is only permitted on official sites. Tavernas, which are a particular feature of Greece, are perfect for the footloose traveller, offering simple accommodation but a very warm welcome.

Greece is a country for many visits, but fortunately there are regional centres, and if one of these is selected then touring about locally presents no great difficulty.

From Athens it is possible to visit many sites in Attica, Marathon, Piraeus, the country's main port, and up to Mount Lycabettus, which gives a good view of the city, and out into Attica to Delphi and through Corinth into the Peloponnese. The trip out to Cape Sounion to see the Temple of Poseidon is particularly fine, and for an island visit, Hydra, in the Saronic gulf, is not too far away.

Delphi goes back to very ancient times but the visitor today will want to see the Byzantine paintings in the church there. Near here

Left: *a fresco in the Byzantine church in the Agora, the ancient meeting-place which developed slowly in the 6th century B.C. as the main square of Athens.*

Rising some 500 feet above sea level, the awe-inspiring Acropolis overleaf is the focal point of the city's antiquity.

the Persian Emperor Xerxes sat on his golden throne to observe his hoped-for victory in the sea-fight at Salamis, so the views are obviously superb, and the traveller can pass on from Delphi to Thebes and the hinterland.

Corinth is ideal for the Peloponnese, and Corinth was, in its day, the first city of Greece. Here one should see the Corinth canal, the Temple of Apollo, the site of Mycenae, and the original Olympic Games, and, of course, Sparta. There are splendid castles, the Byzantine town of Mistra, and apart from beautiful views over the seas, the wide vista of the Argive plain.

The islands, and many visitors to Greece rush directly to the islands, are established in convenient groups. All are worth exploring and the normal way to get about is to take a ferry boat between the islands, and hire a car or moped when you land. A full driving licence is necessary. Ferry boats ply between all the islands and are a novel and exciting way of getting about, and the hydrofoil service, where it exists, is extremely quick. In the Aegean, Delos, birthplace of Apollo, is just perfect and excellent for visits to many other islands in the Cyclades, of which twenty-four are inhabited. Getting about in Crete is a little difficult for there is no railway, no ferry and a complicated bus service.

In the Northern Aegean, Lesbos, or Mytilene as it is sometimes called, is a good place to stop, while Samos, a little off the usual route, is the place for lovers of good wine.

Hydra is the most convenient island to visit from Piraeus, but Poros and Spetses are almost equally picturesque, and a cruise of the Saronic gulf should be included in any visit to Athens.

In the Dodecanese, Rhodes is the largest island and well worth a prolonged visit, but to get a little off the beaten track why not go to Cos, home of the lettuce, or Leros, an island famous for sponge divers, or Patmos, the most holy island in the group, where St John the Divine was martyred in AD 95. The Church and Monastery of St John on Patmos is superb.

To the east of the mainland, in the Southern Adriatic, lie the Ionian Islands, Corfu, Paxoi, Ithaka, Zante, Levkas and Cephalonia, all beautiful and very different from the islands of the Aegean. Corfu is the obvious centre but the smaller islands could well attract the more adventurous traveller, although a devastating earthquake in the 1950s, which fortunately spared Corfu, destroyed much of the old attractions of the other islands. The French once owned Corfu, and the British took the islands in 1807 and held them until 1864. Corfu is a large island and to get about the wise traveller hires a moped and buys a shady hat. Paxoi is only six miles long, Levkas has the castle at Santa Maura, and Ithaka was the home of Odysseus. How is that for choice?

Crete, the main island apart from Corfu and Rhodes, is also worth exploring, with Herakleion as the ideal base. From here the wanderer can visit all the Minoan sites and abandon motorised transport for a trek to Mount Ida, where fierce-eyed Cretan shepherds still tend their flocks, and will welcome visitors who have braved the passage of the *'wine-dark sea'*.

Travelling in Greece is great fun. It helps to have a good phrase book, a friendly nature and a lot of patience, but given these, getting about in Greece is in itself the perfect holiday.

SIGHTS TO SEE

European history effectively began in Greece, and as the basis for modern thought and classical styles in architecture, the Greek influence is profound, and in Greece many memorials of the Classic age still exist in situ, or are preserved in museums. This, in fact, is part of our problem, for Greece is full of sights to see. The vastness of the choice is such as to bring visitors back to Greece again and again. So where shall we begin?

Let us start in Athens, and stop first at the National Archaeological Museum in Pattission Street. This is the finest museum for Greek art in the entire world. It contains the gold treasure excavated by Schliemann at Mycenae, including the golden mask of Agamemnon and, in progressive order, examples of Greek art from the Archaic era, through the Classical and Hellenistic and finally to the Roman periods. The museum is crowded in summer and closed on Mondays, but making a first stop here is useful as well as interest-

ing, for from this point you can decide on your own tastes and go where your fancy takes you. No visitor would leave Athens though, without a visit to the Acropolis and the Parthenon, the temple of Athena, the wise goddess who was the guardienne of the city, and a tribute to Themistocles. The Parthenon is the most perfect example of the Doric style, and was designed by Pericles in about 440 BC. The Acropolis cannot really be described in words, it has to be seen.

A little way from Athens lies Marathon, site of the great battle against the host of Xerxes, King of Persia, while to the north lies Delphi and further north still, the monasteries of Meteora. Across the canal, in the Peloponnese, are many reminders and ruins dating from the time of the city-states. Corinth is just such a place, and the temple of Apollo there, and the amazing narrow slit of the Corinth canal which was begun by the Emperor Nero, are two sights which every visitor will want to see. The Peloponnese is a region to tour, echoing everywhere examples from each historical period as well as the legendary past.

The Greek gods and goddesses had their home on Mount Olympus (9,570 ft.) in Thessaly. There is skiing here in winter on Mount Pelion. Volos is a good centre and the capital of Thessaly, but this is a new town, the former capital having been destroyed by an earthquake, but as a centre for Mount Pelion, and for views of Mount Olympus, which is rarely climbed, Volos is ideal.

The island groups – Ionian, Sporades, Dodecanese – are all beautiful and must be visited which, since the islands within any group are all linked by ferry boat, is not too difficult. Delos, Mykonos, Hydra – all are beautiful – but for history lovers two islands are supreme and count above all others in a list of sights to see.

Crete exerts its own pull, and the Cretans, if fiercely Greek, are primarily Cretan. Crete is full of antique remains, Prehistoric settlements, Roman ruins, and most of all the Minoan palaces at Knossos where, according to legend, the fearsome Minotaur once roamed. Zeus himself was born on Mount Ida. The museum at Herakleion is the largest in Greece, full of treasures excavated from the palace at Knossos, which dates from 2,000 BC and was excavated by Sir Arthur Evans, an English archaeologist. There are other sites on the islands from the Minoan period, at Phaistos and Agia Triadha. It is worth remembering that the 'Spanish' painter, El Greco, was born in Crete.

To the east, and from a much later period, lies Rhodes, the Isle of Roses, capital of the Dodecanese. This island is full of Hellenic remains, classical temples, and in the main town, the great fortress of the Knights of St John, home of the Military Order of the Hospital for hundreds of years from 1309 until they were expelled by the Turkish army led by Suleiman the Magnificent in the sixteenth century. The Street of the Knights contains the palaces of the various branches or *Langues* of the Order, and the great hospital reminds visitors that the first Rule of the Order was to care for the needs of *'Our Lords the Sick'.*

But, in the end, how can one briefly describe the sights of Greece? Start at the National Museum of Athens and go on from there, to Rhodes or Crete, to see Delphi and the Monasteries at Mount Athos (unless you are a woman). See the memorial to the Spartans at Thermopylae, and the Acropolis in Athens. See the mediaeval ports of the Ionian islands, the harbours in the Saronic Gulf, the ruined temples on the hillsides, and the treasures that crowd every museum. When you are tired of looking, you still cannot have seen it all.

SHOPPING

Everything in Greece can be traced back to the past, and so all the best shopping and worthwhile souvenirs have antique links with a past famous for its craftsmen. You can, of course, buy a great deal of junk, and the sponges sold by the street vendors in Constitution Square

Octopus drying outside a tavern in Mykonos left, *a popular town on the Cyclades' island of the same name, which also serves as the departure point for Delos.*

In its magnificent setting stands the Theatre at Delphi overleaf, built in the 4th century B.C., later restored by Eumenes 11 in 159 and later still by the Romans.

never seem too successful when you get them in the bath back home, but if you shop around there are well-made products available at attractive prices. In the larger cities, such as Athens, Corinth and Thessaloniki, the shopping is unlimited, but the street markets and the smaller islands are the best places to find souvenirs which still look attractive at home.

Rhodes produces gold, silverware and good pottery. Mykonos still supports a number of weavers, and the artistic community has produced a good range of products in leather, as well as much indifferent painting. Levkas, in the Ionian islands, has beautiful lace and embroideries, and the other islands have straw-ware, handbags and silver trinkets. Kalamata is famous for silk, while the region of Ioannina has excellent silver trinkets. Copperware, antiques – not *antiquities,* which are protected and require an export licence – leather goods and pottery, are available throughout the country.

Greece is proud of her handicrafts, and there is a showroom of folk art and crafts, organized by the National Handicrafts Organization at the Museum of Popular Art in Athens, which has branches in all the major towns and islands, where handmade Greek craftware can be purchased at reasonable prices. Casts and copies of some exhibits in the National Archaeological Museum are also available. Although Greece is usually and correctly regarded as a warm country, it can get very chilly indeed, and Greek furs are famous for their quality and are available in the shops around the Sindagma district of Athens.

Out on the islands, the shopping reflects the industry of the local people, and can range from such simple items as pistachio nuts, which are delicious, and jars of olive oil, to a wide range of ceramics, leather goods, woodcarving, pottery and handicrafts. The variety is surprising, and differs from island to island.

Embroidery and weaving are always popular in country districts, and so is pottery. Crete's artifacts reflect the influence of the shepherds, who offer good leather ware from sheep hides, woodcarving, and pottery in the Minoan style, Skyros, in the Sporades group, is particularly noted for handicrafts, with hand-carved furniture, basket-work, rugs, stools, chests and embroidery. The architecture of Skyros is also very pleasing to the eye. Skopelos is famous for prunes and almonds, and the nuns of the island convents produce beautiful textiles for skirts and blouses on handlooms.

On Rhodes, apart from silverware, the ceramics come in a wide range of designs and colours, while in Samos the locals produce clay pipes and toys that the children will enjoy. For something even more unique, the islanders of Lesbos (Mitilene) produce special water jars, or *koumaria,* which keep the water cold even in the warmest weather.

Then, for the visitor who enjoys tasty food, there are such pleasures as fresh olive oil, fruit, cheeses, hams and fish from the sea.

One of the major attractions for the visitor, especially those visiting the smaller islands and catering for themselves, are the food-shops. Shops open very early, but shut in the hot afternoons for a siesta, the normal hours being 7.45 a.m. to 1.15 p.m. and then from 5.00 p.m. to 8.00 p.m. Shops shut early on Wednesdays and Saturdays, but these closing times and hours do not affect the small kiosks which dot the towns and villages of Greece and, apart from newspapers and cigarettes, stock a vast range of household items. Haggling over the price is not usual in Greece, but a reasonable offer is usually considered, especially in the street markets and the smaller shops.

EATING AND DRINKING

Even its most fervent admirers cannot describe Greece as a gastronomic paradise but, if the height of classical cuisine must be scaled elsewhere, there is good food in Greece, and the prices are extremely low indeed.

That said, Athens has some great international restaurants; the Xinoa Taverna is excellent, and near Piraeus is the little port of Turkolimano, which is famous among lovers of seafood for its fish tavernas, serving lobsters, octopus and all kinds of shellfish – any gourmet passing through the area must stop here for a meal. In Athens the best restaurants are found in the area known as the Plaka, below the Acropolis, which is always thronged with tourists, but very good value. The whole Plaka district is filled with little bars and food stalls, ideal for a quick snack.

Traditionally, or when doing it as the locals do, the evening begins over a glass of ouzo, and usually a bottle of wine. Retsina, the usual resinated wine, is excellent when chilled, and for ordinary use, *Domestica* is very popular and available everywhere. Typical dishes include *dolmathes*, (meatballs wrapped in vine-leaves), *moussaka*, (a sort of Greek shepherd's pie with aubergines) *stifado*, (stewed veal with onions) *taramosalata*, (fish roe with olive oil and lemon) *tsatsiki*, (yoghurt with cucumber) plus a score more dishes like *pastisado*, *kebabs*, and a whole range of fish and shellfish. The Greeks say you should eat their lamb from Christmas to Easter, veal from Easter to October and pork at any time. Most Greek cheeses come from goats' milk and the vegetables include aubergines, courgettes, tomatoes and artichokes. *Pitti* or pancake bread with a spicy filling is a good cheap snack.

The tavernas, which are best imagined as a bar with cheap accommodation, also have restaurants, and taverna meals are always inexpensive and usually very good, for the taverna owner and his family will eat the food themselves. A meal in a taverna begins with *mèze*, served on a saucer and consisting of anchovy, *féta*–or cheese–egg, and taramosalata. Chips come with everything!

Food in Greece is also highly regional, and if much of the 'Greek' food found outside Greece is, in fact, native to Cyprus, within Greece the range of local dishes is considerable. There are Balkan influences in the region of Salonika; the Italians have made their presence felt gastronomically in the Ionian Islands and the Dodecanese, and the Turks have infiltrated the kitchens of Western Greece and the Peloponnese. All is still Greek, however, and if you eat what the locals eat you will do very well. The seafood is good and found on all the islands. Try the lobsters, the red mullet, and the octopus, all dishes rarely found at home, and excellent with a chilled glass of Samos wine. The beer is more expensive than wine and not particularly good, *Fix* being the major local brand.

The Greeks enjoy their food and like to know what is being done to it behind the kitchen door, so that diners can and do choose their meal by walking into the kitchen and selecting a dish straight from the pot. It is also accepted to order some dishes which the diners then share among themselves, and if you are offered a portion from somebody else's plate, then accept it with a good grace.

A meal without wine is a day without sunshine, and the Greeks, although not great drinkers, have some very acceptable wines.

Retsonia comes white or *kokineti*, a red resinated wine, barrels of which line the walls of most tavernas. The wines of Samos are particularly pleasant, and any meal is usually introduced and ended with a glass or two of *ouzo*. Sweets and puddings reflect the Turkish influence, and *baclavam*, a pastry filled with honey, nuts and spices, is particularly delicious. Ice cream is popular, while to round off the meal, a piece of Greek (Turkish) Delight and a cup of Greek (Turkish) coffee is always available. A glass of water with the meal is essential to the Greek digestion, and the meal will also include, as a standard item, a green salad and some fruit.

Greece has a wide variety of fresh fruit and, not surprisingly, most of the food is cooked in olive oil, which, to reduce the oiliness is mixed with a liberal application of lemon juice and herbs.

The food in Greece is rich, filling and satisfying, wonderfully cheap and always served with a smile.

THE PEOPLE AND THE PAST

To visit Greece and not see the sights which link modern visitors to historic characters would be a very great pity. Much has been preserved from remote antiquity, and places of legend and romance still exist here in great numbers.

Mount Olympus, of course, was the home of the gods, the seat of Zeus, but a more lasting memorial may be found at Olympia, in the Peloponnese, where the Olympic Games were held in his honour. The Games began in 776 BC and lasted until well into Roman times. The modern Olympic Games began in 1896. In ancient Greece they took place every five years, not every four as now, and in the spring time the valley of Olympia, where the Games took place, is cool, green and sublime. The statue of Zeus, in the temple, was one of the Wonders of the World, and the remains of his temple and that of

Hera his wife still remain.

Thermopylae has always been a route for armies. Xerxes came this way after defeating the gallant Spartans, and at Marathon a large mound contains the remains of those Greeks who fell in the great land battle which saved Athens after Thermopylae. Alexander the Great marched across the pass in 480 BC on his way to Persia. Alexander came from Macedonia and Thessaloniki is still the capital of a land much greener and more fertile than the hot south, and is today the second city of Greece. Thessaloniki is known particularly for relics of the Roman occupation, but it was founded by the sister of Alexander.

The south though, and notably the Peloponnese, is the land we think of when we think of the 'city-state', that democratic system of government, envied, destroyed and then briefly emulated by the Roman Republic. Delphi, north of Athens, is another evocative place, the playground of the gods. It stands on the southern slope of Mount Parnassus and overlooks the bay of Corinth. At the base stands the grove of Apollo, a site which, to the antique world occupied the same place as Jerusalem or Compostella in the later Christian era. The Greeks believed that Delphi was the place where Earth and Heaven met, the navel of the Universe. The valley of Delphi today is deeply wooded, full of ruins, and a necessary visit. In the museum of Delphi, among other treasures, stands the famous statue of the Charioteer, dating from 487 BC, as well as treasures from the city of Sikyon.

Athens, of course, is a must for the Acropolis and Parthenon, a tribute in stone to Pericles and Themistocles. The Acropolis survived the Middle Ages as a fortress, but a mine explosion during the Turkish siege of 1687 wrecked the buildings and left then in the ruins we see today.

Rhodes, in the Dodecanese, has many traces of Hellenic times, but is chiefly noted for relics of the Knights of Malta, who lived there for 250 years and built huge and beautiful fortifications.

Among the islands, Delos has to be visited for it combines legend with Classical architecture, and was so sacred to the Greeks that neither birth nor death were allowed there, and in 423 BC, to further preserve the holiness of the island, all the inhabitants were forcibly removed. Hera, the wife of Zeus, persecuted her husband's lover, Lebo, here, setting the island adrift, and Poseidon, god of the sea, is said to have fixed Delos in place with his trident.

Lesbos, or Mitilene, was the home of the poetess Sappho, and Aristotle lectured there at the School of Philosophy. Skyros, in the Sporades, has relics of several empires, Roman, Venetian and Byzantine, and is a very beautiful island.

Back on the mainland, the ancient theatres – notably the Theatre of Dionysus and the Odeon at Athens – where the works of the great Greek playwrights, Aristophanes, Sophocles, Euripides, were first performed, still stand among the olive groves, and the works of the masters are still regularly re-enacted there. You may need to understand Greek to get the best out of it, but the drama itself is superb.

Countless civilizations have settled in Greece for long or short periods, from the Dark Ages to the present day. Greece has seen the Persians, the Dorians, the Romans, the Byzantines, the Turks, the Venetians, and even the British. All have left their mark, and in any part of the country, some relic of their occupation will still remain. In the end though, these were transitory visits, and the visitor will be mostly concerned with, and interested in, those places which relate to the Greeks themselves. If you want to see their monuments, just look about you.

The glittering white houses and small church right *reveal the special charm of Mykonos, whilst* overleaf *the majestic Parthenon stands as a symbol of Classical Greece.*

In contrast to the broad sweep of modern Athens, seen in the panorama above, stand the ancient remains of a glorious past. Like the charming little Temple of Athena Nike below in the Acropolis, the graceful columns of the Parthenon top and bottom left are of Pentelic marble. Below the Acropolis is the Odeon of Herodes Atticus right, and centre left, close to the Agora, the Horologium of Andronicus of Cyrrhus, or Tower of the Winds.

Beautiful Hydra overleaf rises in an amphitheatre on the precipitous hills that enclose its deep, natural harbour.

Delphi, built on the slopes of Mount Parnassus, was the spiritual and religious centre of ancient Greece. Within the sacred site the Tholos above and below; *the Temple of Apollo* left and top right, *and the Stadium* centre right *vividly evoke its Classical past. At Cape Sounion the Temple of Poseidon* bottom right *commands the highest point of the headland, and overleaf is a view towards Galatas, on the Peloponnesian coast, from Poros.*

31

Vouliagmeni above is Attica's most fashionable seaside resort. Aegina, seen across its modern harbour above right, *stands on the small, triangular island of the same name. One of the principal excursions from the town is to the splendid Temple of Aphaia* left, *which perches on a pine-clad hill above the Saronic Gulf. Pashalimani Harbour overleaf is separated from the Great Harbour of Piraeus by an isthmus, while farther east, below the hill of Kastella, is the smaller, busy harbour of Tourkolimano* right. *The Stoa of Attalos* below *stands at the eastern edge of the Agora in Athens.*

34

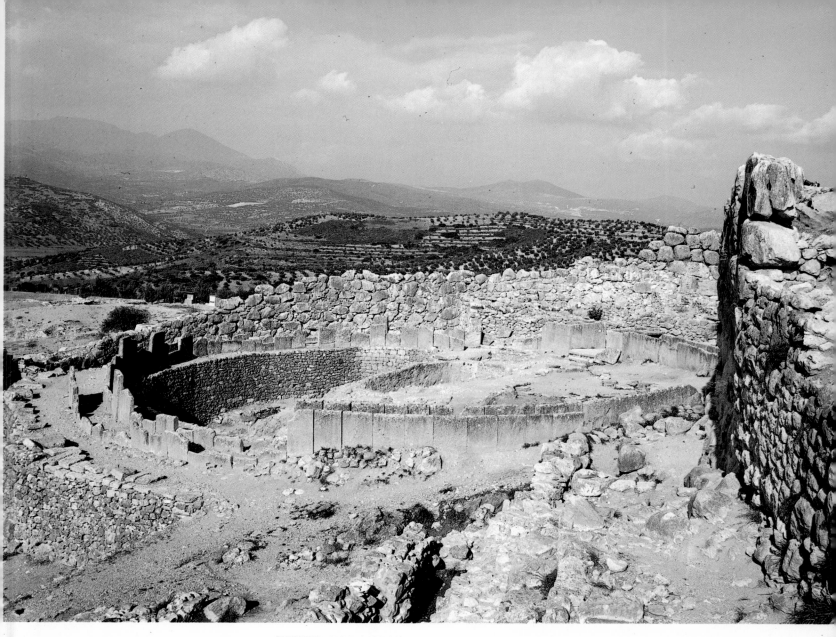

The Peloponnese is renowned for its captivating scenery and splendid archaeological remains. In the tree-studded mountain region lies picturesque Langadhia *left, which appears to tumble down an outcrop of rock above the valley, and the Gorge of Lousios and hamlet of Lefkokhori *right. In the western Peloponnese is the sacred precinct of Olympia *overleaf, and in the northeast the famous citadel of Acrocorinth *below.

Called by Homer a city 'rich in gold', ruined Mycenae *above is traditionally known as the capital of Agamemnon.

The six kilometre-long Corinth Canal right cuts through the narrow isthmus of Corinth, linking the Aegean Sea with the Gulf of Corinth, and thence with the Adriatic and Italy. The idea of cutting a canal through this narrow land bridge which links central and northern Greece with the Peloponnese, thus saving shipping the long and often arduous journey south around Cape Matapan was a very old one. Although the existing canal was built by a French company between 1882 and 1893, both the ancient Greeks and the Romans had produced plans for one.

Ancient Corinth lay on a rocky plateau below the northern slopes of the mountain of Acrocorinth between its citadel and the sea. A flourishing commercial centre, the city's importance as a trading centre between Asia and Europe was due to its commanding position between two seas, and its prosperity was further enhanced by the Isthmian Games held in the neighbourhood every other year. The site is rich in archaeological interest and among its extensive remains are the statues in the museum above, and the Temple of Apollo below, one of the oldest in Greece, dating from between 550-525 B.C.

South of Corinth lies New Epidauros top left, the little harbour of which is used by the ferry service from Piraeus, and the ancient city of Epidauros centre left – once a religious centre and fashionable spa. Its superb theatre overleaf is the best preserved of all Greek theatres and a festival of drama is held here each summer.

Close to the ancient site of the Olympic Games stands the spacious International Olympic Academy in its magnificent setting bottom left.

Across the rooftops of Nauplia – the capital of the nome of Argolis, and a popular seaside centre – lies the islet of Bourdzi top left, on which perches the 15th-century Castel Pasqualigo. Offering superb bathing facilities from Xenia Beach centre left, this attractive town is crowned by the crags of Its-Kale, from where can be seen unparalleled vistas of the rocky peninsula right. Methoni, in Messenia, with its soft, sandy beach below, is a small fortress town that still retains its ancient fortifications bottom left. North of Methoni is the magnificent natural harbour of Navarino above, below Pylos, and overleaf Skiathos, the island capital of the Sporades group.

Euboea, or Evvia, is, next to Crete, the largest
Greek island, extending for almost one hundred
miles parallel to the mainland, from which it is
separated by a strait, virtually landlocked at either
end. Its cosmopolitan pleasure spots, contrasted
with tranquil, secluded coves make it an ideal
summer venue. Above left *can be seen* Edipsos;
below left *Agiokabos, and* above and right
Limni.

Greece is renowned for its superb sandy beaches
such as Lalaria on Skiathos *below and*
Mirtiotissa *overleaf, on the beautiful Ionian
island of Corfu, which, combined with sparkling
summer sunshine draw holidaymakers from all
over the world.*

51

Parga these pages, *a picturesque seaside town backed by olive and orange groves, spreads across the neck of a rocky headland opposite the island of Paxos. Its tiny bay reveals rocks, islets and myriad cafés along the waterfront, while the larger bay of Khrissoyiali, a mile to the west, has a magnificent sweep of beach partly occupied by the Club Mediterranée.*

A pale gold sunrise suffuses the horizon and mantles the berthed boats in Corfu harbour overleaf.

One of the seven islands of the Ionian Sea, Corfu, with its spectacular sunsets *above left,* holds an almost magical fascination that has persisted throughout the long history of Greece. The most northerly of the islands, it is sited less than two miles off the Albanian coast, and is the closest Greek land to Italy – the effects of its Venetian domination still apparent in a legacy of bi-lingual place names.

Its capital, Corfu, or Kérkira, situated on an irregular peninsula, roughly half way along the east coast, is a busy port of call for steamers, cruise ships and naval vessels, and is a favourite resort of visitors. Between the Esplanade, or Spianada, and the Palaion Frourion is a 16th-century moat *below left,* where motor boats may be hired, crossed by a cannon-flanked bridge.

On the north coast of the island is the secluded cove *above at Sidari,* whilst Paleokastrista on the north-west coast, with its dramatic scenery *below,* is renowned for its breathtaking aquamarine bay *right and overleaf,* backed by tree-studded hills and framed by a profusion of colourful wild flowers.

The sheer beauty of Paleokastrista is pictured above, and left and below the pretty fishing village of Benitzes, south of Corfu, where a crimson sunset hangs above the darkened harbour with its illuminated ferry boat above right.

Nightfall silvers the inimitable Corfu coastline right, its shimmering waters the perfect setting for the charming convent of Vlaherna on its tiny islet, with Pontikonissi (Mouse Island) behind, and seen from Kanoni Point overleaf.

Picturesque white-walled houses right line the enchanting streets of the towns and villages of Corfu. As in Old Corfu left; Sinarades above and below, and Aghios Deka below far right, the charm of the narrow alleys is enhanced by the fragrant blooms and painted shutters that provide a delightful background for the merchandise that is offered for sale in time-honoured fashion.

The Meteora in the mountains of central Greece is famous for its monasteries which date from the 14th century. Like Moni Agios (Varlaam) overleaf, they perch on detached, almost inaccessible pinnacles of rock. Many of the original two dozen monasteries are now, however, derelict.

Of all the sun-drenched islands in the Aegean Sea, Mykonos is probably the most famous. It is a treeless, rocky, but strangely fertile island in the centre of the Cyclades. The town and port of Mykonos right, *with its glittering white houses* above and below left and below *is on the west coast, on the site of an ancient city. Near the water's edge the houses rise straight from the sea* above, *giving this area the nickname 'Little Venice'.*

Overleaf: *The steep, zig-zag path from Skala Fira to Fira, on Santorini.*

Of the many little churches below on Mykonos, built from the proceeds of fishing and piracy, the Church of St Mavri Paraportiani, with its dazzling white exterior *top left, is particularly enchanting. This charming town is also noted for its three celebrated windmills *centre left, and above and below right *which perch on the promontory above the town.

Santorini is a volcanic island in the south Aegean Sea. It is actually only half a volcano now, as the rest split away and sank into the sea during a geological disturbance thousands of years ago. Cruise ships land visitors at Skala Fira and they ascend by donkey along a tortuous road to the town of Fira *above and overleaf *which clings to the clifftops nearly 700 feet above the sea.

Ancient Thera, built on a rocky spine of Mesa Vouno, is known to have been occupied before 2,000 B.C. Called in antiquity Calliste (Most Beautiful), the site is rich in archaeological remains. *Bottom left is shown the Sacred Way.

Fishing on Mykonos, as on all the Greek islands, is an important part of daily life, and as such, fishing boats and fishermen are a familiar sight in the sun-drenched harbour *previous page, bottom left,* and *below.*

Naxos, the largest and most beautiful of the Cycladean islands, is divided by fertile valleys where citrus fruits and groves of olives grow in abundance. Seen from the harbour *top left,* its capital, Naxos, is an ancient town celebrated in legend as the place where Theseus deserted Ariadne on his return to Athens from Crete.

The interior of the Cyclades island of Paros is almost entirely filled by Mt Profitis Ilias, on the slopes of which are the renowned marble quarries. Naoussa *centre left,* in the north of the island, is a pretty fishing village with a small caique harbour, whilst its capital, Paroikia, or Paros, *right* extends along the west coast, backed by distant hills.

Plomari *above* is the second largest town of the lovely Aegean island of Lesbos, and *overleaf* is shown Agios Nikolaos, a fashionable Crete resort, on the west side of the Gulf of Mirabello.

80

Lying across the southern Aegean basin, Crete is the largest and most southerly of the Greek islands. Midway along the north coast is sited Herakleion, the small inner harbour of which *top left* is guarded by a 16th-century Venetian fortress. At the north entrance, the giant pithos *above* stands amid ruined remains. A superb panorama towards Agios Nikolaos is shown *centre left*; *bottom left the Plain of Lasithi with its countless windpumps; above right the north end of the Samaria Gorge,* and *below right a view towards Laki.*

Lying not far from Herakleion, Knossos, the Minoan capital with its splendid palace, was first inhabited at the beginning of the New Stone Age. Extensive excavations at the palace include the Throne Room *above* and the Hall of Colonnades, the south-west corner of which can be seen *below.*

Clustered around its beautiful bay is Simi *overleaf, on the lovely Dodecanese island of the same name.*

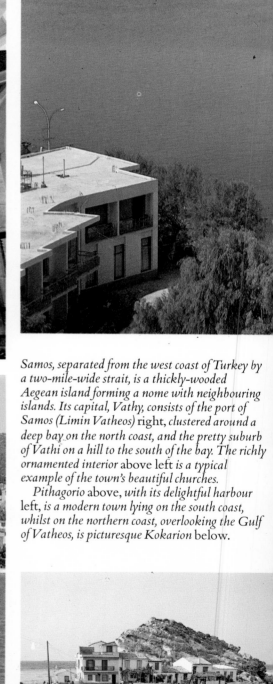

Samos, separated from the west coast of Turkey by a two-mile-wide strait, is a thickly-wooded Aegean island forming a nome with neighbouring islands. Its capital, Vathy, consists of the port of Samos (Limin Vatheos) right, clustered around a deep bay on the north coast, and the pretty suburb of Vathi on a hill to the south of the bay. The richly ornamented interior above left is a typical example of the town's beautiful churches.

Pithagorio above, with its delightful harbour left, is a modern town lying on the south coast, whilst on the northern coast, overlooking the Gulf of Vatheos, is picturesque Kokarion below.

The enchanting island of Rhodes, the capital of
the Dodecanese, is strategically placed in the
eastern Aegean. The fortified city of Rhodes was
built by the Knights of St John, and the Old City,
hemmed in by the 500-year-old walls that encircle
the Commercial Harbour *top left*, still retains its
mediaeval appearance. The new town stretches
along the waterfront of Mandraki, its harbour
entrance guarded by the famous bronze deer *right*.
Government House *left* is a modern building in
Gothic and Renaissance architectural styles.

The village of Lindos *overleaf* is built on the site of
one of the three ancient Dorian cities of Rhodes. Its
venerable Acropolis, sited on a triangular outcrop of
rock, is approached by the mediaeval entrance
below. Part of the Great Stoa is shown *above*,
and *bottom left* part of the large Doric Stoa.